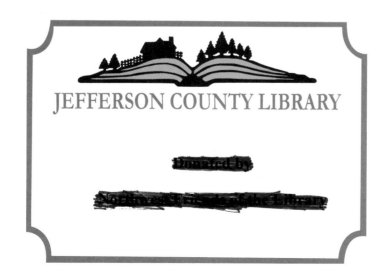

DEMI LOVATO

★ SINGING SENSATION ★

Big Buddy Books
An Imprint of Abdo Publishing
abdopublishing.com

BIG BUDDY POP BIOGRAPHIES

KATIE LAJINESS

abdopublishing.com

Published by Abdo Publishing, a division of ABDO, PO Box 398166, Minneapolis, Minnesota 55439.
Copyright © 2018 by Abdo Consulting Group, Inc. International copyrights reserved in all countries.
No part of this book may be reproduced in any form without written permission from the publisher.
Big Buddy Books™ is a trademark and logo of Abdo Publishing.

Printed in the United States of America, North Mankato, Minnesota.
092017
012018

THIS BOOK CONTAINS
RECYCLED MATERIALS

Cover Photo: Rich Fury/Getty Images.
Interior Photos: Alberto E. Rodriguez/Getty Images (p. 15); Andrew H. Walker/Getty Images
    (p. 13); Christopher Polk/Getty Images (p. 23); Jason Merritt/Getty Images (p. 17); Jesse Grant/
    Getty Images (p. 21); Joe Scarnici/Getty Images (p. 27); Kevin Winter/Getty Images (p. 5);
    Larry Busacca/Getty Images (p. 25); Mark Davis/Getty Images (p. 11); Rich Polk/Getty Images/
    Turner (p. 19); Rick Kern/Getty Images (p. 29); ZUMA Press, Inc./Alamy Stock Photo (p. 9).

Coordinating Series Editor: Tamara L. Britton
Contributing Editor: Jill Roesler
Graphic Design: Jenny Christensen

Publisher's Cataloging-in-Publication Data

Names: Lajiness, Katie, author.
Title: Demi Lovato / by Katie Lajiness.
Description: Minneapolis, Minnesota : Abdo Publishing, 2018. | Series: Big buddy pop biographies |
    Includes online resources and index.
Identifiers: LCCN 2017943937 | ISBN 9781532112164 (lib.bdg.) | ISBN 9781614799238 (ebook)
Subjects: LCSH: Lovato, Demi , 1992-.--Juvenile literature. | Singers--Juvenile literature. |
    Actors--Juvenile literature. | United States--Juvenile literature.
Classification: DDC 782.42164092 [B]--dc23
LC record available at https://lccn.loc.gov/2017943937

CONTENTS

SUPERSTAR

Demi Lovato is a talented actress, **pop** singer, and businesswoman. First known as an actress, Demi has become famous for her big voice.

Demi is popular around the world. She has been **interviewed** on television shows. She has also appeared on magazine covers. And fans love her music!

SNAPSHOT

NAME:
Demetria "Demi" Devonne Lovato

BIRTHDAY:
August 20, 1992

BIRTHPLACE:
Albuquerque, New Mexico

POPULAR ALBUMS:
Don't Forget, Here We Go Again, Unbroken, Demi, Confident

FAMILY TIES

Demetria "Demi" Devonne Lovato was born in Albuquerque, New Mexico, on August 20, 1992. Her parents are Patrick and Dianna Lovato. Shortly after Demi turned two, her parents **divorced**.

Her mother later married Eddie De La Garza. Demi has three siblings. Her sister Dallas and half sister Amber are older than she is. Demi also has a younger half sister, Madison.

DID YOU KNOW?
Demi and her sisters grew up near Dallas, Texas.

WHERE IN THE WORLD?

Utah

Colorado

Kansas

Arizona

Oklahoma

Albuquerque

New Mexico

Texas

MEXICO

GROWING UP

As a child, Demi knew she wanted to **perform**. She started in **beauty pageants**. Her first television **role** was on *Barney & Friends*. After the show ended, Demi began taking guitar and piano lessons.

Growing up, Demi had a hard time in school. Kids were mean to her, so she began homeschooling instead. On set, Demi studied between scenes.

At eight years old, Demi was crowned Texas State Cinderella Miniature Miss.

DID YOU KNOW?

Demi met pop star Selena Gomez at the audition for *Barney & Friends*.

9

RISING STAR

Demi wanted to **audition** for more TV shows. So, her family moved from Texas to Los Angeles, California. For her next major **role**, Demi joined the cast of Disney's *As the Bell Rings*.

She continued to earn Disney roles. In 2008, Demi starred in *Camp Rock* with the Jonas Brothers. In this TV movie, she showed off her powerful singing voice. Next, she played the lead character on *Sonny with a Chance*.

Demi and Selena Gomez starred in the 2009 Disney Channel Original Movie *Princess Protection Program*.

Already a successful actress, Demi still dreamed of being a **pop** star. In 2008, her dream came true. Demi **released** her first album, *Don't Forget*. It sold about 500,000 copies.

Demi and the Jonas Brothers returned in 2010 for *Camp Rock 2: The Final Jam*. Fans loved Demi's voice. So, she joined the Jonas Brothers on tour.

DID YOU KNOW

In 2009, Demi finished high school a year early!

Minnie and Mickey Mouse posed with Demi at the premiere of *Camp Rock 2: The Final Jam*. About 8 million viewers tuned in to watch the sequel.

BIG COMEBACK

Life as a superstar was hard. Demi reached a point where she needed help. So, in late 2010, she left the *Jonas Brothers Live in Concert* tour.

Demi spent three months at a clinic. There, she learned a lot about herself. She wanted to live a healthier life. After **treatment**, Demi was ready to return to the stage.

14

During her struggles, Demi leaned on her family for help. Her half sister Madison helped Demi heal.

POP PRINCESS

Demi made a major comeback in 2011. She **released** her third album, *Unbroken*. It featured her hit song "Skyscraper." The song reached number ten on the *Billboard* Hot 100.

She returned to TV in 2013 when she appeared in the **musical** series, *Glee*. Demi played a character named Dani in four **episodes**. The show was wildly popular with millions of viewers.

Demi (*right*) appeared on *The X Factor* for two seasons.

Demi was very successful in 2016. She sang a **duet** with country singer Brad Paisley. "Without a Fight" received more than 7 million views on the website YouTube.

She joined Nick Jonas on the *Future Now* tour. Together, they **performed** across North America.

DID YOU KNOW?

Demi was on *The Tonight Show Starring Jimmy Fallon*. She showed off her talent for copying other artists.

Demi joined Brad Paisley onstage at the iHeartRadio Music Awards in 2016.

SOCIAL MEDIA

Demi has been very active on **social media**. As of 2017, she had more than 43 million followers on Twitter.

About 58 million Instagram followers enjoyed seeing Demi's photos. On Facebook, she had nearly 38 million followers. Today, fans still love to know what Demi is doing.

To promote their concert tour, Demi and Nick Jonas let fans on Twitter decide what they should eat. The two stars ate baby food!

AWARD SHOWS

As a **pop** star, Demi has attended many **award** shows. Together with Brad Paisley, Demi sang "Stone Cold" at the 2016 iHeartRadio Music Awards. She also **performed** at two different **Grammy Award** shows!

Demi has won many awards for her music. She has taken home People's Choice Awards and multiple Teen Choice Awards.

Demi performed at the Grammy Awards in 2016 and 2017.

GIVING BACK

Demi has spent time giving back to many worthy causes. She has worked with groups that help fight illness and support children, women, and the arts. Demi has also **performed** at concerts to raise money for **charity**.

In 2016, Demi attended a benefit for the Metropolitan Museum of Art in New York City, New York.

BUSINESSWOMAN

Demi has been a successful businesswoman. She started a makeup, skincare, and clothing line. She has written a book. *Staying Strong: 365 Days a Year* became a bestseller. In the book, Demi shared how she lives a healthy life. She has used **social media** to **promote** her products.

In 2013, Demi met fans at a Barnes & Noble bookstore in Los Angeles, California. There, she signed copies of her book.

BUZZ

In 2016, Demi traveled to Kenya with a group that teaches job skills to women. Then, in 2017, she announced that she was taking a break from the spotlight.

Throughout the year, Demi attended special events and made a few TV appearances. Fans are excited to see what Demi does next!

Demi sang at the Concert for the Causes in Arlington, Texas.

GLOSSARY

audition (aw-DIH-shuhn) to give a trial performance showcasing personal talent as a musician, a singer, a dancer, or an actor.

award something that is given in recognition of good work or a good act.

beauty pageant (BYOO-tee PA-juhnt) a contest between a group of girls or women that often includes a showing of beauty, talent, and character.

charity a group or a fund that helps people in need.

divorce to legally end a marriage.

duet a song performed by two people.

episode one show in a series of shows.

Grammy Award any of the awards given each year by the National Academy of Recording Arts and Sciences. Grammy Awards honor the year's best accomplishments in music.

interview to ask someone a series of questions.

musical a story told with music.

perform to do something in front of an audience.

pop relating to popular music.

promote to help something become known.

release to make available to the public.

role a part an actor plays.

social media a form of communication on the Internet where people can share information, messages, and videos. It may include blogs and online groups.

treatment medical or surgical care.

ONLINE
RESOURCES

Booklinks
NONFICTION NETWORK
FREE! ONLINE NONFICTION RESOURCES

To learn more about Demi Lovato, visit **abdobooklinks.com**. These links are routinely monitored and updated to provide the most current information available.

INDEX